MOUNTAIN REFLECTIONS

When we see the alpine ptarmigan white in winter, the red-grouse the colour of heather, and the black-grouse that of peaty earth, we must believe that these tints are of service to these birds in preserving them from danger. Hence I can see no reason to doubt that natural selection might be the most effective in giving the proper colour to each kind of grouse.

Charles Darwin,
The Origin of Species,
1859

MOUNTAIN
REFLECTIONS

KEITH BROCKIE

Meall Odhar (830 m/s)
3r4th June 92

MAINSTREAM
PUBLISHING
EDINBURGH AND LONDON

ALSO BY KEITH BROCKIE
Keith Brockie's Wildlife Sketchbook *(Dent, 1981)*
One Man's Island *(Dent, 1984)*
The Silvery Tay *(Dent, 1988)*

ILLUSTRATED BY KEITH BROCKIE
The Puffin *by M. P. Harris (T. & A. D. Poyser, 1984)*
Studies on the Tihamah *edited by F. Stone (Longman, 1985)*
The Sparrowhawk *by I. Newton (T. & A. D. Poyser, 1986)*
The Kestrel *by A. Village (T. & A. D. Poyser, 1990)*
The Status of Seabirds in Britain and Ireland *by C. Lloyd,*
  M. L. Taser and K. Partridge (T. & A. D. Poyser, 1991)
The Great Wood of Caledon *by H. Miles and B. Jackson*
  (Colin Baxter, 1991)

First published in Great Britain in 1993 by
MAINSTREAM PUBLISHING COMPANY (EDINBURGH) LTD
7 Albany Street
Edinburgh EH1 3UG

ISBN 1 85158 557 5

A catalogue record for this book is available from the British Library

Typeset in Souvenir Italic by Saxon Graphics Limited, Derby
Printed and originated in Singapore by CS Graphics Ltd

Introduction

To the uneducated eye mountain uplands look bare in comparison with lower elevations but, in truth, their whole surface contains a wealth of biological detail and is a rich tapestry of shapes and textures. Specialised montane birds and animals reflect these patterns – hence the title for this book.

The process of drawing teaches one to observe a subject anew and to take in all its subtleties of colour, light and shadow. Sketching wildlife in the field demands a unique harmony of eye, mind and hand in which consciousness becomes a purposeful stream of energy. For me the pinnacle is a wonderful tranquillity, like a life force drawing its strength from the act of communication with the subject facing. It is essentially a very private, even selfish occupation because one has to concentrate totally on the subject and disregard all interruptions and random thoughts. Companions receive short shrift. However, as soon as the bird or animal I am drawing departs, the spell is broken and I return to reality. I can only hope that I have captured on paper something of that special moment.

Nature has always exerted a powerful magnetism on me and I have tried to respond to this by reproducing in this book some of my personal experience of fieldwork in the bleak but beautiful mountain landscapes of my native Scotland. Threading their way through the book are the seasonal life rhythms of two species, the rock ptarmigan and the mountain hare, and the ways in which they have adapted to a harsh environment. For many years I had been contemplating an intimate, artistic study of a single species rather than another general collection of work such as in my three previous books. Hares are a favourite species of mine, with their expressive faces, full of character, and I never tire of portraying them. Artistically, however, the idea of combining them with the ptarmigan increasingly began to take shape in my mind and present an irresistible challenge. I knew it would be a difficult project because these two species occupy a

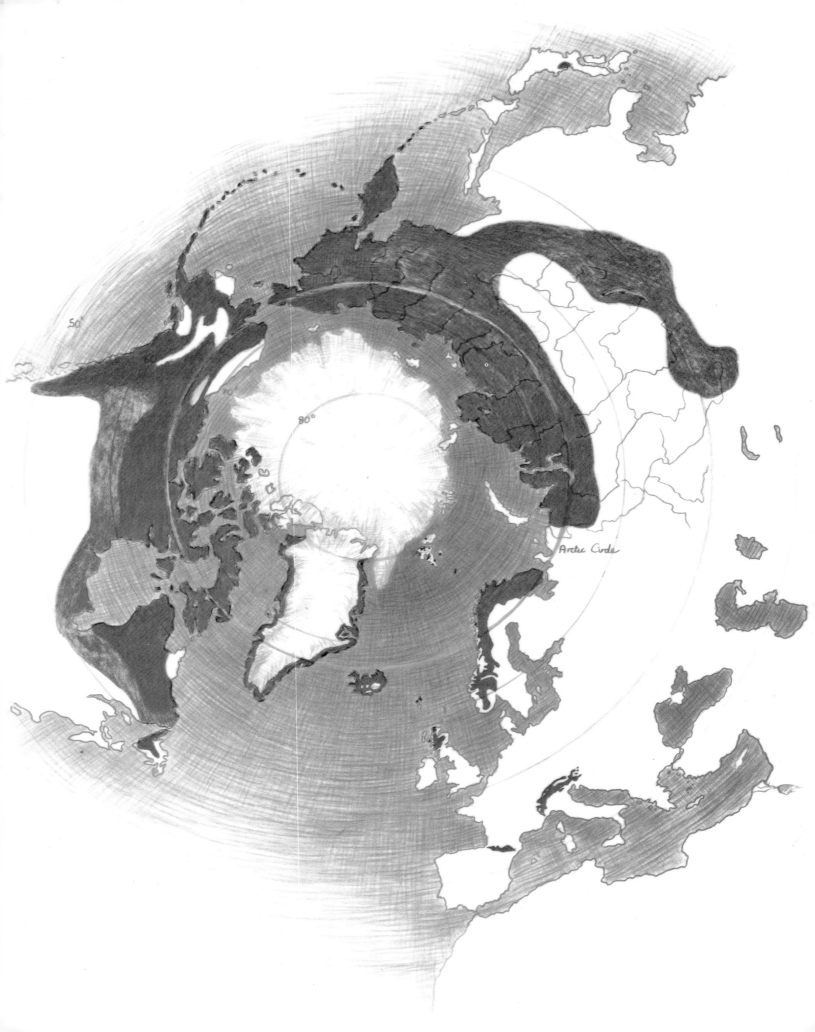

Arctic Circle

terrain which is completely exposed to the vagaries of the climate. Nevertheless, I also knew that nothing similar had been attempted before and that it would be a real contrast to my previous work. I have also included other mountain wildlife – not only from Scotland but also from Greenland – so as to give a more diverse picture of the flora and fauna inhabiting these levels.

Relatively few people have seen ptarmigan, apart from hillwalkers and skiers who venture into their domain. Many will have passed close by without realising the birds were there, sitting tight, relying on their superb camouflage to avoid detection. On misty days, strange ventriloqual croaking calls emanating from the hillside give away their presence. I think my earliest encounter with ptarmigan was when I was 15 years old. I was hillwalking on An Teallach, Wester Ross, and came upon a female with a brood of chicks. As I leaned down to pick up a chick to have a closer look the whole brood exploded into the air in all directions whilst the mother performed a distraction display around my feet. It was hard to believe those tiny balls of down could fly short distances at such an early stage of their development.

The rock ptarmigan Lagopus mutus is a medium-sized grouse about 35 centimetres in length, with a wing span of 54 to 60 centimetres, and weighs around 500 grammes. It is the only British bird which turns white in the winter months. Adult Scottish ptarmigan go through three distinct body plumage phases — from winter to spring/early summer, then to late summer/autumn before turning back to winter, with transitional patterns in between. The timing of the moult varies greatly according to the individual, its sex, the altitude and weather conditions, but generally the birds start moulting from their white winter coat to their spring plumage from late February to early May. The cock birds are more advanced than the females, which catch up in April, moulting very quickly from a few new feathers to almost complete summer plumage in around 20 days. The summer/ autumn moult from June to early September is the most complete; the birds turn to a greyer, finely marked plumage and renew their wing and tail feathers. From late September to November they change back to their white winter plumage, with the hens now usually more advanced than the cocks.

The rock ptarmigan has a circumpolar distribution from sea level at the highest latitudes in the sub-Arctic through the middle latitudes to high mountains in the Arctic-Alpine zone. As the map (page 6) indicates, it is found in the Pyrenees, the Alps, Scotland, the Faroe Islands (where it was introduced), Iceland, Scandinavia, Northern Siberia, Japan, Alaska, Canada and Greenland. Some 20 or more sub-species are recognised, though most of my work in this book is from the Scottish race L.m. millaisi. Lagopus, a compound of the Greek words lago and pous meaning 'hair' and 'foot', is an appropriate name since the legs and toes of the ptarmigan, particularly during the winter months, have a thick feathering which acts both as thermal insulation and as a form of snow shoes, enabling the bird to spread its weight on soft snow. Mutus means 'silent', and applies since the rock ptarmigan is usually less vocal than the other main Lagopus species — the willow ptarmigan, L. lagopus. Within the British Isles this latter species is represented by the red grouse, L. l. scoticus which has evolved without white wings and white winter plumage. Although the range of the red grouse on the hills overlaps with the rock ptarmigan the two species seldom mix. The only other Lagopus species is the *white-tailed ptarmigan* L. leucurus *which is found in the Rocky Mountains in North America.*

Since the 1800s the range of the British rock ptarmigan has contracted from the Lake District, south-west Scotland and the Western Isles, most probably because overgrazing by sheep has degraded the botanical diversity of the upland plant community. The rock ptarmigan is now confined to the Scottish Highlands — mainly above 600 metres' altitude but down to 200 metres in northern Sutherland. Research by Adam Watson and others has shown that the Scottish ptarmigan population may be cyclical, with peaks roughly every decade. Numbers vary according to the time of year, but the winter population after a reasonable breeding season is probably between 10,000 and 30,000 birds.

Rather more people will have seen mountain hares than rock ptarmigan because of their much wider distribution, particularly in mild winters when their white pelage stands out against the brown moorland heather. They can be fairly tame and, although they will bound away when disturbed, they often stop after a short distance. The mountain hare Lepus timidus *is smaller and stockier than the brown hare* Lepus capensis, *with shorter ears and no black on the upper tail. Scottish mountain hares have a body length of around 50 centimetres and weigh about three kilograms when fully grown. They are found on moorland over most of the Scottish Highlands and have been introduced to some of the Western Isles, Orkney, Shetland and the Scottish Lowlands. The well-managed grouse moors of north-east Scotland, with their more nutritious vegetation, support the highest densities of mountain hare. South of the border there are declining populations in the Pennines and North Wales. In Ireland the mountain hare is represented by a distinct sub-species,* L.t. hibernicus, *which in summer has a redder pelage and in winter has a piebald appearance with either a few white patches or none at all. Worldwide, mountain hares are found in the Alps, Faroes (introduced), Iceland, Scandinavia, the boreal and tundra zones of Siberia, and Hokkaido in Japan. In the Nearctic tundra region are found the closely related Arctic hare* Lepus arcticus, *tundra hare* L. othus *and snowshoe hare* L. americanus.

As with the ptarmigan, the seasonal moult of the Scottish mountain hare varies greatly with the individual. The start of each moult appears to be fairly uniform but progression can be checked or hastened by factors such as age, altitude, length of daylight and prevailing weather. Generally the mountain hare moults from white to brown (mid-February to late May), brown to brown (early June to mid-September) and brown to white (mid-October to December). Many do not become fully white, especially at lower altitudes, and retain brown on the face, ears and back. Other names for the mountain hare include the blue hare (due to a bluish tinge to the summer coat), white hare (relating to its winter coat) and varying hare. Apart from the stoat no other British mammal turns white during winter.

My fieldwork was mostly carried out above the 700-metre contour in the area surrounding the Glenshee ski centre on the boundary between the counties of Perthshire (Tayside Region) and Aberdeenshire (Grampian Region). The main road peaks here at 655 metres which facilitates access to the hills. This is the nearest ptarmigan habitat to my home, an hour's drive of some 40 miles (or 29 as the ptarmigan flies). As the Gaelic derivation of their names indicates, the surrounding mountains are fairly unspectacular – Cairnwell, 933 metres (hill of bags – referring to the pouchy peatbanks on the slopes); Carn Aosda, 917 metres (hill of age); Meall Odhar, 922 metres (tawny lump); and Glas Maol, 1068 metres (greenish-grey bare hill). But the underlying rock of Dalradian schists and quartzites supports a rich heath of heather, blaeberry and crowberry, with extensive Nardus grassland and rock scree and, despite being scarred by a web of ski-tows, snow fences and related infrastructure, the mountains are rich in wildlife, including a high density of breeding rock ptarmigan and mountain hare.

Although there is skiing in the winter months (when conditions permit), and a chairlift operates in summer to take tourists almost to the top of the Cairnwell, from which they can view the surrounding landscape and from which regular hang-gliding events take off, the base rich vegetation recovers well from these depredations in comparison with other ski centres in Scotland. Tourists and hillwalkers generally keep to the paths, so disturbance to the area's wildlife is minimal. Unleashed dogs are one of the main problems, particularly in the early summer when wild creatures, with their young, are more vulnerable. Whilst painting one day on Meall Odhar I watched with amusement the incongruous sight of two dachshunds chasing hares around the hill slopes and scree, followed vainly by their owner who tried to keep pace and retrieve his dogs. This lasted for nearly an hour but the hares were always too swift to be in any danger.

As a contrast to Scottish wildlife I have included a number of paintings and sketches which I made on two expeditions to the Mestersvig area of eastern Greenland. There I studied at first hand a different sub-species of the rock ptarmigan and the Nearctic equivalent of the mountain hare –the Arctic hare – which, in Greenland, stays white all year round. Also included are species such as musk ox, Arctic fox, collared lemming and snowy owl which have adapted in different ways to the harsh Arctic environment.

A telescope is an indispensable aid for field sketching with animals and birds. For longer walks into the hills I carried a habicht 30 × 75 telescope with a light tripod (see photo, page 5). Mostly I used a Questar field telescope with a 50 to 80 times magnification eyepiece. The large 89 millimetre object lens lets in a great deal of light, giving a sharp and bright image with no chromatic aberration in the fringes. (Heat haze can be a problem on sunny, windless days – but there are not too many of them in the Scottish mountains!) One quickly becomes accustomed to the reversed image of the mirror lens. Paired with the adaptable Benbo tripod this telescope affords comfortable working positions in all manner of terrain. The combined weight can be a drawback but their solidity in windy conditions more than compensates. Looking down through the questar's eyepiece, with the paper directly below the telescope, enables me to view and sketch a subject with the minimum of distracting movement of the head and eyes. It allows me a smoother, quicker flow from subject to paper.

As readers of my books will know, I do not usually paint from photographs. On this occasion I had no choice but to use photography as an aid with my fieldwork on the ptarmigan. The principal reason was that the complicated cryptic summer and autumn plumage of the ptarmigan would have necessitated impossibly lengthy periods of *observation as well as placing undue stress on the birds, particularly the incubating females. With photographs I could avoid these problems and render the camouflaged plumage patterns in the comfort of my studio. Likewise, photographing chicks as they developed saved me precious time during the busiest periods of the year, when I had many other subjects to sketch in the mountains. Trying to draw accurate plumage details even from my captive chicks would be hard enough when they were small, but next to impossible as they grew up and their feather patterns became ever more complicated. However, there is no substitute for actually watching and sketching the subject in the field for, without first-hand experience, one cannot really paint from a photograph with any feeling or conviction. Only hours of observation can properly imbue an artist with a deep understanding of the species involved.*

The depiction of the stages of growth of known-age chicks was a crucial element in this book. Attempting this with wild broods would have been impossible given the triple problems of locating chicks of the exact ages required, excessive disturbance and unreliable weather conditions. So I found a nest where the female was laying up and took the eggs just as she had completed her clutch. Losing them at such an early stage of incubation meant that she would lay another clutch soon afterwards – this happens regularly in the wild when predators steal the eggs. I then transferred the clutch to a broody bantam hen which I had been keeping for just this eventuality. She hatched six of the eight eggs –another died in the egg just prior to hatching and the last was infertile. One chick died at 12 days, but the hen successfully reared the remainder. I kept a daily record of their wing length and weight as they developed. I gave two to an aviculturalist and kept the other three until November that year, when a stoat got into their pen and killed them. By then, however, the ptarmigan were almost white and I had secured a useful record of the progression of their moult from precocial down, through juvenile plumage, to the first winter coat.

Other sources of reference were a series of ptarmigan corpses, casualties of the ski-tow wires on days with low cloud or mist, and a representative series of mountain hares, killed by vehicles on the main through-road, which provided me with excellent insights into their pelage detail, colouring and texture, which I kept in a freezer.

The fieldwork for this book was spread over several years because I knew from past experience that the unpredictability of the weather would always be the final arbiter as to what I could achieve in such an environment. The mountains have a micro-climate all of their own; often I would set out in fine weather from my home only to find the hills shrouded in low cloud or a persistent wind blowing. The contrast between the same months in different years can be quite stark. For example, June 1991 began with a snow storm and freezing temperatures which lasted for a week, and continued with such fierce wind and rain that I was driven to distraction. June 1992, however, was superb with sunny weather and hardly a drop of rain – though this caused problems of a different kind, such as plants going over very quickly. Winter conditions can prove equally problematic with very little snow falling in some years (to the chagrin of the skiing fraternity more than me). Climatic differences nevertheless add character to the story, and the extended timescale at least allowed me a leisurely approach so that I did not have to panic about missing suitable material during spells of bad weather. I could also thoroughly familiarise myself with the species in order to preplan what I wanted to illustrate. The sketching practice made subsequent fieldwork easier and more natural, and I hope the resulting paintings will afford the reader as much interest and pleasure as they have given me.

Species such as the golden eagle, peregrine falcon and dotterel are specially protected under the Wildlife and Countryside Act 1981. Within Scotland appropriate licences from the Scottish Natural Heritage must be obtained to disturb these birds during the nesting season. Gamebird eggs such as the ptarmigan's can only be legally taken with the keeper/landowner's permission.

I worked on this project over a number of years and I would especially like to express my thanks to the following: Stuart Rae for his help and companionship on the hill whilst doing his PhD on ptarmigan; Bill Bain, keeper/stalker with Invercauld Estate, on whose beat I did most of my work; Adam Watson, research scientist, who has spent much of his life studying ptarmigan; Dave Patterson of the Glenshee Chairlift Company; the British Schools' Exploring Society for organising the Greenland expedition; Steve Moyes (page 5) and Pete Moore (below) for the photographs; Peter Shellard for his work as agent and editor.

Last but not least my thanks are due to my wife Morag for putting up with unreasonable hours and dark moods during inclement weather.

During the winter months, conditions permitting, hares use snow holes like this one on the Cairnwell (January 1991). They provide safe refuge from hunting eagles and shelter from the elements in this extreme environment. The snow hole was dug out under an overhanging cornice in the lee of prevailing westerly winds.

A fox hunting on the slopes being buffeted by spindrift on a windy day. The fox is one of the primary predators of the mountain hare and ptarmigan.

The well-defined ptarmigan tracks in the powder snow, above, show
the indentation of toe pads and claw-drag marks. Opposite and
below, the tracks break through a thin, icy crust over deep snow, the
low light and shadow giving them more 'depth'. In deeper snow the
feathered toes act like snowshoes to spread the weight.

A stoat in its February coat, mostly white with only a little brown on the head. The mountain hare and stoat are the only British mammals regularly to turn white during the winter months. It is beside a ptarmigan trail made earlier while the snow was softer.

By early March brown fur is starting to appear on the head and back, though many hares, particularly at lower elevations, keep some brown throughout the winter. During daylight they remain higher on the hill and come down lower to feed during the hours of darkness. This hare was sitting on a ridge on the Cairnwell, the snow sculpted by the wind into beautiful patterns highlighted by the low angle of the sun.

I have always been attracted to hares by their wonderful facial expressions – they exude character, like old wrinkled men. This one was dozing and soaking up the warm sunshine in a snow hollow on the Cairnwell. Above, now in shadow, the hare is alert to an approaching skier off the main piste.

*Mad March hares: mountain hares may not be so extrovert as brown
hares at this time of year but small parties come together to joust,
box and chase each other in aggressive display.*

Cairwell

Meall Odhar

February 88

*A male ptarmigan in mid-song flight, sailing in the strong updraft,
Carn nan Sac in the background. In song flight the cock flies up into
the air, sails momentarily with wings and tail outspread before
fluttering down with tail fanned and head and neck outstretched.
During the sailing and descent he issues 'belching and cackling' calls
and continues the display on landing, strutting about with tail
fanned. This display is most frequent between February and May
when the territorial cocks are most active. The height of the flight
indicates how dominant he is.*

A male ptarmigan displaying on his territory to dissuade other cocks from encroaching. This one, on 1 April 1990, is already well advanced in his spring moult. The 'combs' above the eye play an important part in display. The colour is particularly vivid and when he is excited they swell up with blood to become even more prominent.

Mountain hares can produce three litters of two or more leverets between March and August. The leverets are born fully active after a gestation period of around 50 days. Initially the mother feeds them on milk once a day during the hours of darkness. Small young usually remain hidden in holes amongst scree, in vegetation or in forms and burrows in the peat. Occasionally they can be found in fairly open positions on exposed ridges and plateaux. This tiny leveret was crouching motionless at 870 metres amongst lichen-encrusted quartzite and woolly fringe moss.

♂ chasing off an intruding ♂
with his ♀ in attendance

♂ in threatening posture, combs very
prominent

This incubating female was sequinned with raindrops from a recent shower which glinted with the colours of the spectrum.

Ptarmigan nests are often found beside stones or in a depression amongst vegetation. Some nests, on the lower slopes down to 680 metres, are well concealed amongst long heather more typical of a red grouse nest site, though most are in fairly open positions. Both the male and the female make nest scrapes and the hen starts laying her eggs at daily or two-day intervals. The shallow scrape is loosely lined with grass, lichens and usually some breast feathers. Clutch sizes vary from three to 12 eggs depending on the condition and age of the bird. In good years clutches normally number around seven or eight eggs. The eggs usually have a cream or rose-tinted background heavily marked with dark-brown blotches. Prior to incubation the female conceals the incomplete clutch with a thin layer of vegetation. Only the female incubates, for some 21 to 23 days from the last or penultimate egg. Once incubation has started she does not bother to cover the eggs when she comes off, three or four times a day, to drink, defecate and feed. The main threat to the eggs in this area is from foxes, stoats, weasels, ravens and common gulls, but if the eggs are lost to predators early on during the incubation the female will often lay another clutch elsewhere. During incubation the cock ptarmigan guards the area from some prominent perch overlooking his territory. When the female comes off to feed he comes down to escort her until she returns to the nest.

The clutch opposite is the one I took to hatch out under a bantam hen in my garden. The nest was by a long stone which had a quartzite zigzag which almost seemed to point to the clutch. Curiously the clutch had a non-pigmented egg which was positioned next to the white quartzite. Pale eggs are not common and this one hatched out successfully.

Only a very deep fall of snow would trouble this hardy bird, Meall Odhar, 3 June 1991. Summer snowfalls seldom lie for more than a few days, but during this particular period of bad weather the snow was covering the ground down to 600 metres altitude.

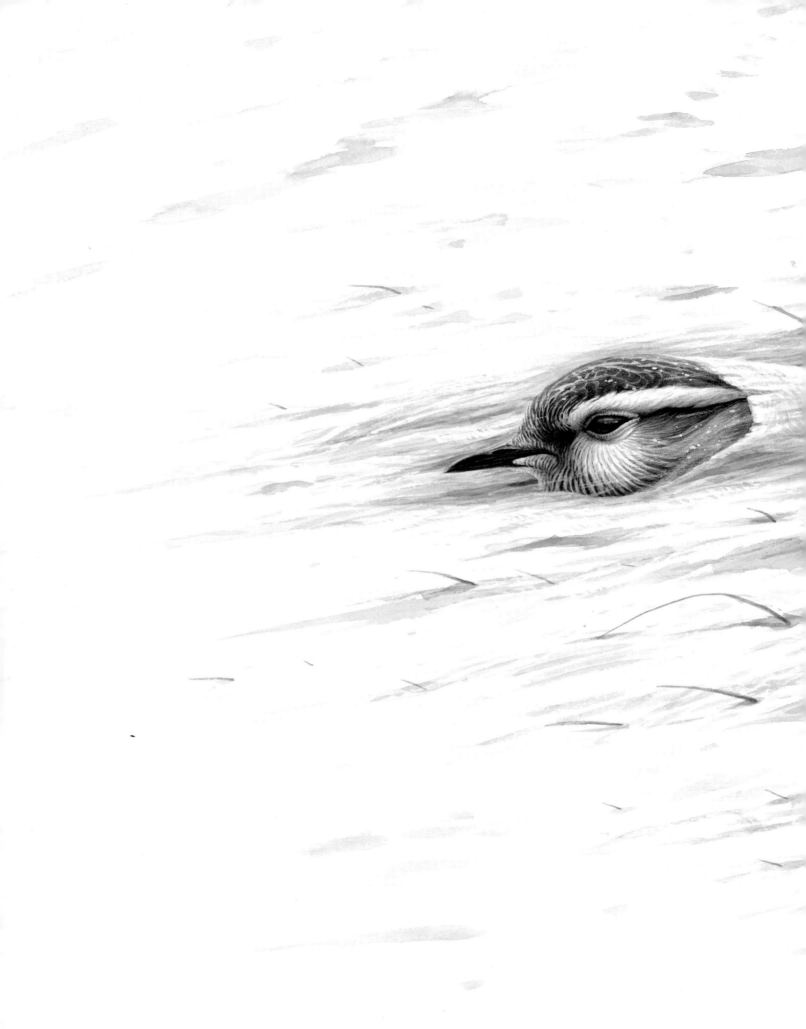

This male dotterel must have remained on its eggs for at least three days during the appalling weather at the beginning of June 1991. I observed him at 1,000 metres' altitude. He looked relatively insulated under a coating of icy snow and was probably in a semi-torpid state in order to conserve energy: there was no point in his coming off the nest to feed because all the feeding areas were similarly covered and an exposed nest scrape would have been quickly filled with spindrift. The grass stalks were already coated with a thin wedge of ice. Despite the prevailing conditions the dotterel managed successfully to hatch the clutch, and he was later seen with one young fledgling.

This tiny young leveret had a harsh baptism on the mountains. I found it right on the summit of Glas Maol one day in June exposed to the full ferocity of the wind and driving snow. There was no shelter on the rounded summit and it was crouched with its back to the wind and coated with spindrift. Conditions had been like this for days and it was a miracle that it had survived thus far.

A male ptarmigan surveying his territory near the summit of Meall Odhar in June 1992. The summit of Carn Aosda is to the near left, the valley of Glen Clunie and the Cairngorm massif are on the horizon.

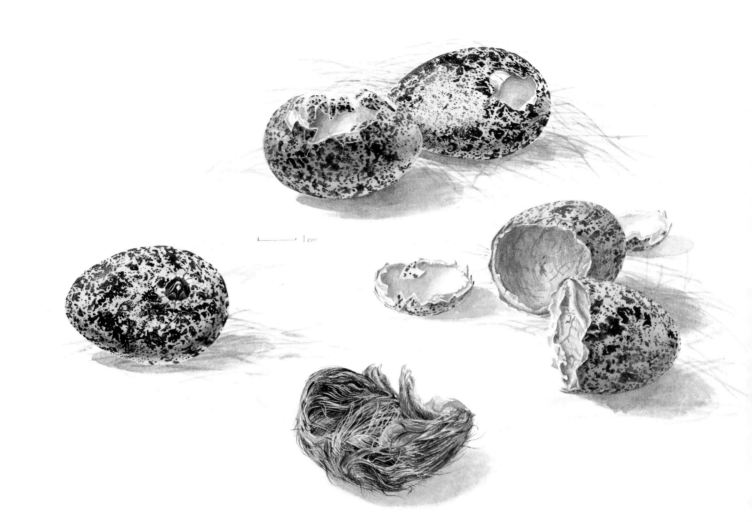

Clockwise from the top are two predated eggs, two hatched eggs, a chick which died just before hatching and a 'chipping' egg. The predated eggs are recognisable from the pierced shells and yolk stains on the inner membrane. Hatched shells have a fairly even cut around the top end of the egg and the loose membrane shows traces of blood vessels. The membrane from the eggshell cap has a clear, off-white colour where the air cell is situated within the egg. The emerging chick uses an 'egg tooth' on the upper mandible to chip off the egg cap. On the left-hand egg you can see the chick's bill starting this process.

Opposite is a brood which has recently hatched, including one chick which has just come out and whose down is still wet. Chicks weigh around 16 grammes at birth; they are precocial which means that they are active immediately after hatching. Hatched egg shells are left in the scrape. Successful nests from the previous year are still recognisable the following spring from fragments of shell and membrane on the lining which are not yet obscured by emerging vegetation. The brood usually leaves the nest with the female within 12 to 24 hours of the first chick hatching.

Newly hatched chicks are becoming more adventurous, peering out from behind their mother's wing and clambering on her back as she pants in the sunshine.

Opposite is a group of one-day-old chicks at rest. After three days (above) they have lost the egg tooth from the bill and are much more active. They usually feed themselves, mainly insects for the first week and vegetation thereafter.

Nine-day-old chicks feeding amongst vegetation, including some flowers of dwarf cornel which is common in this area. Since birth the chicks have doubled in weight to 32 grammes. Juvenile feathers are now appearing through the precocial down, and the primaries, secondaries, greater coverts and scapulars are clearly visible. By now the chicks are switching from an insect to a vegetarian diet.

16 day old chick 1/1

By 16 days there is quite a change in the young, their weight having increased to around 55 grammes. Most of the wing feathers are out now and the back and flank feathers are just starting to show. This one was standing in a herb-rich wet flush, at 870 metres altitude on the Cairnwell slopes, containing some attractive plants such as frog orchid, Scottish asphodel and Alpine meadow-rue.

24 days old

22 days old

29 days old

Meall Odhar (830 m's)
3 r 4ʰ June 92

The cloudberry, a relative of the bramble, grows on damper ground amongst mosses and other vegetation. It does not hold its petals for long. Wind and rain soon strip them, so I have to paint them quickly. The fruit which develops (see page 118) is red initially before turning a golden-yellow colour when fully ripe. They are much prized, especially in Scandinavia. Also in flower is the blaeberry on the left, prior to turning into a delicious blue-black berry. Other plants include stiff sedge and crowberry amongst some grouse droppings.

Ptarmigan enjoy dust-bathing in hollows on bare patches of soil, as well as in snow and water. These chicks are 37 days old and their plumage is progressing quickly.

*The 46-day-old chicks stretching their wings and legs.
They usually stretch these limbs on one side at the
same time. The moult of the wing from juvenile to first
winter feathers is well advanced, as is the new tail.*

typical first year, more pigment on P9 than P8

9 8

8
9

typical adult

53 days old, about to moult last juvenile primary

primaries 9 & 10 growing
at same time as
inner ones.

33 days old,
new primaries growing well.

19 days old, juvenile carpal remex coming through now, two possible
functions of this odd feather are (a) to protect the new primary
feathers coming in underneath it at the moment or (b) to help
camouflage the white feathers coming in.

8 days old

Progression of juvenile to first winter wing of Rock Ptarmigan
(all roughly life size)

Juvenile P8 stopped growing

3	4	5	6	7	8	9	10	11	12	13	14	15	16	17	18	19	20	21	22	23	24	25	27	29	33	36	39	42	45	48	51	54	days old
25	28	36	39	42	49	55	56	60	65	69	73	76	80	84	87	90	95	100	103	108	112	117	125	132	145	157	164	168	171	174	180	-	mean (of 5) wing length mm's
16.8	19.3	20.6	24.2	25.7	28.7	32.0	34.9	37.2	40.0	43.9	49.8	55.4	61.4	65.8	72.4	79.0	86.0	93.0	100.8	108.2	119.6	129.2	150.6	170	209	242	268	299	319	352	366	395	mean weight - gm

extent of primaries when fully grown

red grouse ⅟₁

rock ptarmigan ⅟₁

moulted juvenile carpal remex

new 1ˢᵗ winter carpal remex
'old' feather moulted at 60 to 65 days old

atypical juvenile ♂ wing, Cairnwell
20ᵗʰ August '92

secondary coming out

Opposite is a 53-day-old chick, well-grown and weighing around 400 grammes, which has started to moult into its first autumn plumage. It was watching a falcon soaring high overhead. By 66 days old, as above, the chicks' juvenile feathers have been largely replaced by autumn plumage and the feet are well feathered.

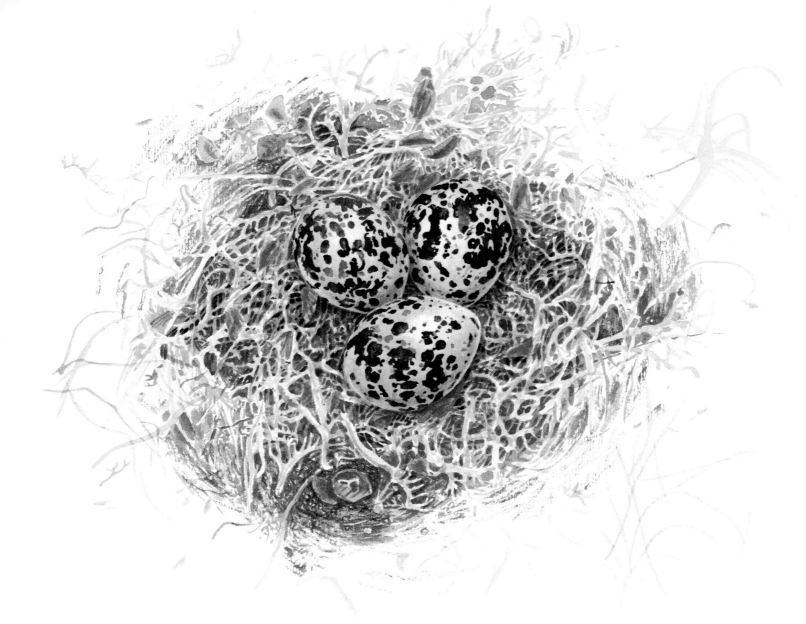

Dotterel nest on high mountain plateaux and 'whaleback' ridges in Scotland. Recent research has shown the population numbers around 800 pairs. They arrive back from their wintering grounds in Morocco usually during the first week of May and laying is well under way by the end of the month. This clutch was on the Hardangervidda Plateau in southern Norway. Ringing has proved that there is some interplay between the Scottish and Scandinavian populations. During the same season a male dotterel which was incubating eggs near Glenshee was subsequently discovered with chicks in Norway, having moved there after his first clutch failed. The usual clutch is three beautifully marked eggs in a nest scrape lined with lichens and vegetation.

Opposite are two dotterel chicks, the upper one only a few days old, the lower half-grown. When alarmed, young chicks lie prone amongst the vegetation, relying on their camouflaged plumage to avoid detection.

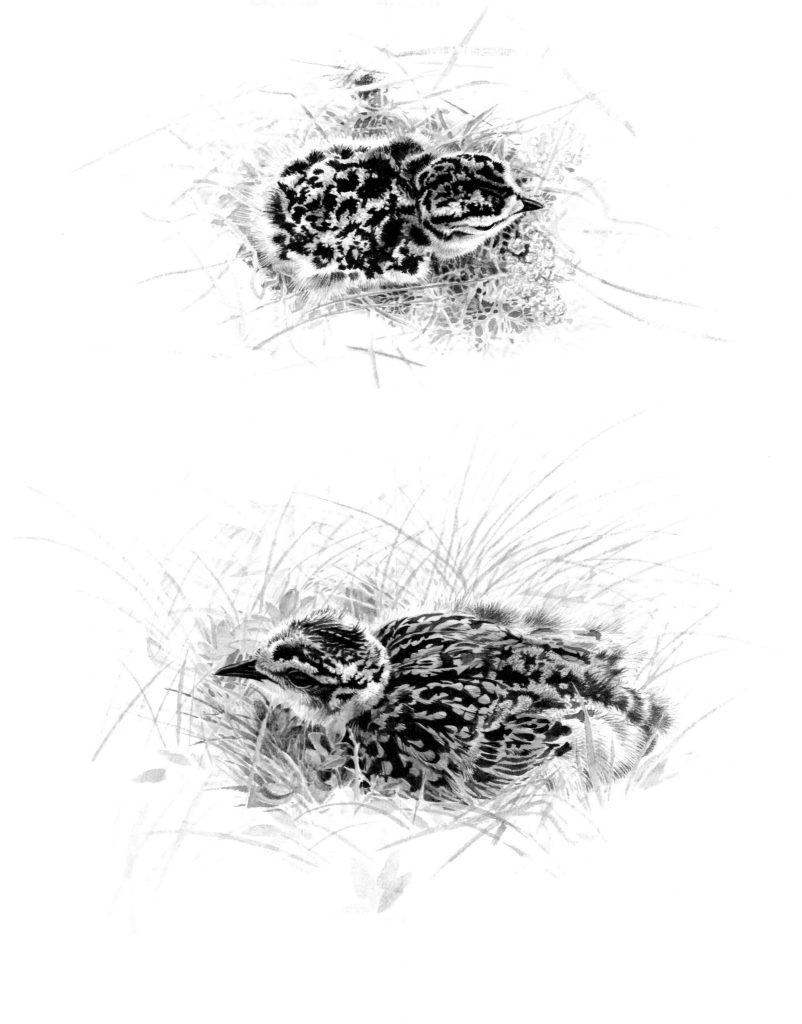

I found this dotterel nest on 1 June 1990 on a hill where they had
never been known to breed before. Ten days later two of the chicks
had hatched, the last was chipping out of the shell and the oldest
chick was already starting to make short forays away from the nest.
The female lays the eggs then disappears, leaving the male to
incubate the eggs and rear the chicks all on his own.

I came across this freshly dead red deer calf on 15 June 1991 whilst
searching for calves amongst the grass and heather. Young calves
are often quite obvious from above because their spotted coats are
much less well camouflaged on the hillside than they are in the
dappled woodland setting which is their normal habitat in other
countries. I took this calf home and worked on the painting for a few
days in my studio before the carcass started to go off. This was an
excellent opportunity for a close study of the texture of its coat, the
legs, hooves and head. Research has shown that around 20 per cent
of calves die in their first summer, mostly within the first few days of
life. The bad weather earlier could have been a factor in the death of
this particular calf.

For the first week after the birth of her calf, the hind leaves each morning for the upper hill slopes and summits where she can keep troublesome flies at bay. She returns in the evening to suckle her youngster which has remained curled up, motionless, amongst the vegetation. After a week or so the calf is strong enough to follow its mother on to the slopes.

This calf had just been born when I spotted the hind eating the afterbirth. It was six o'clock on the morning of 10 June 1992. I waited a couple of hours till the hind had gone up on to the hillside before moving in to sketch the calf.

Red deer calf, a few days old.

Keith Brockie '92

red grouse chicks, newly
hatched. one chick was
very dark
6th June 92
Meall Odhar

11 to 12 days old red grouse chick
Meall Odhar, 23rd June 91

Red grouse chicks are very similar to ptarmigan chicks but are
generally darker. One of the newly hatched chicks above was very
dark in comparison with its siblings.

Unlike the male ptarmigan, the cock red grouse takes an active role
in rearing the young. Opposite, this bird on the Cairnwell slopes was
extraordinarily aggressive. As soon as I had picked up a chick he
launched into the attack. He repeatedly flew up to my head and
tried to strike me with his wings, and only backed off when I beat a
hasty retreat.

threat display

This hare was moulting out the last vestiges of its winter coat, giving it a curious appearance with scattered tufts of long white hair (Meall Odhar, 11 June 1990). Opposite are two pencil field sketches, including the one for the study above.

orange head·
lighter on nape and

pole dull anim background
tufts of white winter coat

lighter sides

11th June 90
Adult - Meall Odhar

Meall Odhar 21st May 89

amongst heather & blaeberry, with droplets of rain
Carnwell

young leverets

Meall Odhar

This is one of two leverets, probably ten to 14 days old, which I found in a 70-centimetre-long peat burrow on Meall Odhar. I made a few quick sketches to work up later before replacing it (June 1990).

Juvenile Peregrine Falcon, just fledged.

2nd year ♀ peregrine falcon, from an escaped falconry
bird which I caught near my house, October 92

remains of a ptarmigan killed by a peregrine showing
characteristic 'notched' sternal keel

coracoid

sternal keel

radius

humerus

sternal ribs

ulna

scapula

Opposite is an eight-week-old male golden eagle chick in his eyrie
which was unfortunately in the shade by the time I arrived. I
sketched the eaglet via a telescope from the hillside overlooking the
eyrie before climbing in and ringing the chick. The remains of prey in
the eyrie had attracted a lot of flies which were annoying the eaglet.
In the foreground lies the remains of a mountain hare's leg. Along
with red grouse and ptarmigan, hares form the majority of the
eagle's diet at this time of year in Tayside. I have only once
witnessed an eagle kill a ptarmigan. One winter's day I was watching
an eagle soaring above the lip of a snow-corniced corrie when it
suddenly dropped to the ground. Next minute, a flurry of white
feathers in the wind signalled the unfortunate demise of a ptarmigan.
Foxes also prey on both the hare and the ptarmigan, peregrine
falcons take fully grown ptarmigan, stoats and weasels take their
young, and kestrels and ravens, given the opportunity, will take very
small young. Man, too, has his influence on the ptarmigan; some 20
per cent of the autumn population have been shot in the Cairnwell
area in recent years, while 10 to 20 per cent die annually by striking
the ski tow wires, particularly when mist or low cloud reduces
visibility. However, this mortality is very localised and immigration
soon takes place from neighbouring hills.

primaries and coverts from a ptarmigan
killed by a fox showing the characteristic
chewed off feather shafts

During the summer, hares are most active in the late evening, the few hours of darkness and early morning. They generally spend most of the daytime lying in forms amongst the vegetation, holes in peatbanks or amongst scree. This one is soaking up the June sunshine in a peat hollow surrounded by vivid blaeberry and wavy hair grass. Opposite is a young hare in the shadow of a snow fence. Hares and ptarmigan can often be found close to fencelines which must provide a sense of security from aerial predators.

An adult male ptarmigan amongst scree in late August on Meall Odhar. Its finely vermiculated autumn plumage blends in extremely well with the surrounding grey lichen-encrusted rocks. At this time of the year he loses his dark eyestripe and at a distance can sometimes be difficult to distinguish from a female. From late June to September the moulting males are usually in groups, occasionally joined by females who have lost their clutches or broods.

♀ upperwing

Arnica alpina

♂ upperwing

Northern Clouded Yellow
Colias hecla ½
Mestersvig, Greenland Aug 91

Greenland

The British Schools' Exploring Society takes parties of young 'explorers' (usually 17 to 18-year-olds) on expeditions to remote places each year, mostly in Arctic climes. I have been fortunate to accompany three expeditions to east Greenland under their auspices, acting in various capacities – group leader and art and wildlife tutor. The last two expeditions in 1988 and 1991 were to the Mestersvig area of Scoresby Land, roughly halfway up the east coast of Greenland at 72° 14′ N, 23° 53′ W. This is a supremely serene, beautiful area. The horizon is crowned with the jagged snowy peaks of the Stauning Alps, and extensive glacier systems, foothills and tundra roll down to the fjord with its drifting pack ice and icebergs. In the distance, across King Oscar's Fjord, lies Traill Island. Living under canvas for six weeks and travelling on foot is the ideal way to savour a wilderness like this in all its moods. One almost becomes part of the landscape and its wildlife.

The restricted range of species found here has adapted well to the extreme environment. My favourite is the musk ox, which looks like an animal which has stood still since time immemorial, completely at one with its surroundings. Some birds and animals, like the Arctic fox, Arctic hare, stoat, collared lemming, ptarmigan, gyr falcon and snowy owl, are white during part or the whole of the year. White coats are not only excellent camouflage but in addition provide superb insulation. The white radiates less heat and the lack of colour pigmentation within the hollow hair/feather structure allows better heat retention. Fortunately there are no polar bears here during the summer to complicate matters.

I also spent some days in 1991 exploring the north of Iceland. Opposite is a young merlin chick in an old raven nest on one of the lava mounds in the Dimmuborgir, by Lake Myvatn. When I found it, in July, this female chick was just about to fledge, while three other chicks were already on the wing.

2♂♂ + 10♀♀ Harlequin. Duck.

Akureyri, Iceland 11th July 1991 on a fast

flowing river near junction with sea

sandy
opaque river

♀

Whilst waiting for an outward flight from Iceland to Greenland with
the advance expedition party I had a chance to explore the coast
around Akureyri. I found a party of harlequin ducks roosting on a
shingle bank where a stream entered the sea. This was the first time I
had ever seen this duck. It is always a challenge to sketch a new
species because you have few preconceptions of what the bird
should look like – you just draw what you see. The sleeping drakes
gave me a splendid opportunity not only to delineate their gorgeous,
abstract plumage but also to study the species at length. Iceland is
the only breeding area for the harlequin duck within the western
Palearctic and I could not resist including these sketches.

Kong Oscar Fjord, Traill Ø, Greenland

© Keith Brockie 16ᵗʰ Aug 1988

Above is a view of Traill Island across King Oscar's Fjord from Nyhavn, Mestersvig, a sand bar separating the shallow bay from the sea. Opposite are some views of icebergs in different weather conditions, one on a drizzly day (you can see where raindrops have hit the paper) and the other with a heavy evening sky. The vast panoramic landscapes of Greenland are magnificent, the incredible crisp clarity of the atmosphere making distance perspective very difficult. One constantly underestimates travelling times. In such a pristine environment I even began to resent intrusions such as the vapour trail from a transpolar jet temporarily scarring the sky. On calm days the awesome, almost oppressive silence is broken only by the occasional birdcall or calfing iceberg. It is so quiet you can almost hear the blood pumping round your head. The summer here is short, and by the end of August 1988 the snow was already settling at lower elevations and sheet ice was forming overnight on calm coastal bays. By then, too, the midnight sun was starting to dip below the horizon giving some fantastic sunsets and sunrises over a superlative landscape.

King Oskar Fjord, Traill Ø, Greenland

© Keith Brockie
4th August 88

King Oskar Fjord

© Keith Brockie 25th August 88

Norway Lemming !,
from Hardangervidda, Norway

The roughly four-year population cycle of the collared lemming controls much of the success and numbers of other wildlife in the area. In years with a high lemming population all the predators take them instead of other species. In turn this leads to higher breeding success rates for birds and the predators themselves. During poor years the predators focus on other species with poorer breeding success for prey and predators alike. I have witnessed lemming peaks in Norway, but as yet have 'mistimed' my visits to Greenland. The 1991 lemming population was low and I had to do the initial sketches from captive animals in the Danish Sirius Patrol base in Mestersvig. During the summer months they live in underground burrows. When the snow comes they build nests from vegetation on the ground surface underneath the snow linked by a labyrinth of tunnels.

Collared Lemming ⁵⁄₄
summer pelage

primary covert

⊢———⊣ 1 cm

Opposite are two moulted feathers, a bleached pellet and pieces of lemming skulls from a mound probably used as a hunting lookout by a snowy owl. Unfortunately, due to the reduced lemming population, there were no owls breeding in the Mestersvig area during 1991; only a single male was present, who did not allow a close approach. The main prey of owls are the lemmings which form the majority of old regurgitated owl pellets of undigested fur and bone. However, the pellet shown here consisted of ptarmigan remains, and you can see the beakless skull to the left end and two claws from the toes in the upper middle portion. Below is part of an ancient reindeer antler encrusted with lichens. Things take a long time to decompose in an Arctic environment and this antler is almost certainly decades old, since reindeer died out in this part of Greenland a long time ago.

A male ptarmigan in late July plumage in a field of boulders with dark lichens. This Greenland sub-species is very brown compared with the grey autumn plumage of the Scottish ptarmigan.

This female ptarmigan was brooding six small chicks at midnight on 20 July 1991. They were quite restless and every so often a couple of chicks would rush out from underneath her to forage for food. The chicks are grey-brown in comparison with the yellow-brown of small Scottish chicks.

A lifesize clump of mountain avens amongst leaf litter. The feathery styles are beautiful when the flower head goes to seed. Opposite is a group of Arctic poppies on a gravel slope. The barren Greenland landscape is studded with Arctic-Alpine jewels, though few exceed 20 centimetres in height because of the harsh climate, and even the trees in the form of dwarf willow and birch grow prostrate along the ground.

Skeldal
11th August 91

These two Arctic hares made a charming study as they sat on either
side of a large boulder. I was particularly fascinated by the play of
light and shadow on their pelage. Whilst sketching this duo I noticed
them becoming tense. I looked up to see a magnificent white gyr
falcon gliding by some 20 metres away and peering closely at me
and the hares. Its curiosity satisfied, the falcon continued on its way
south and the hares relaxed again.

Shaldal 11th Aug 91

Nyhavn
Mestersvig 25th July 91

cassiope

Arctic hare

Arctic hares stretching and grooming

Arctic hares frequently hop along on their hind legs, bodies fully upright, especially when alarmed. This certainly gives them a better view of the surrounding topography and possible predators.

yawning Arctic hare

mountain hare skull ⅟₁

The front incisor teeth lack roots and grow throughout life. A thicker coating of enamel on the outer side means that the inner side wears down more quickly, keeping a sharp chisel edge for cropping the vegetation. The upper set of molars are wider than those on the lower jaw, necessitating a sideways chewing action.

Skeldal, Mestersvig, Greenland, 12th August 91

The Inuit word for the musk ox is oomingmaq, 'the animal with skin like a beard'. It has a wonderful primordial appearance. A dense layer of long, coarse, guard hair hangs down like a skirt. Less coarse hairs form a mane round the head and shoulders. During the summer months the thick, fine underfur is shed in patches and streamers, giving the animal a shaggy appearance. Old males like this one are usually solitary and are seldom aggressive unless overly disturbed by people. The horns have a helmet-like buss over the skull which absorbs the impact when bulls charge each other during the rut. They spend long periods resting, making them ideal subjects for a more detailed field sketch such as this one drawn with the aid of a telescope from a distance.

The dark musk oxen stand out starkly in the vast mountain panoramas, their slow drifting gait and flowing 'skirt' giving them a tranquil, almost oriental appearance.

more rufous

dull, lt. brown

28th July 88

rocks appearing
through snow

The Mestersvig area is nicknamed the 'Arctic Riviera' because it
often has sunny weather during the summer months. This can make
life very uncomfortable for the musk oxen with their thick coats.
They can often be found cooling off by lying on snow patches.

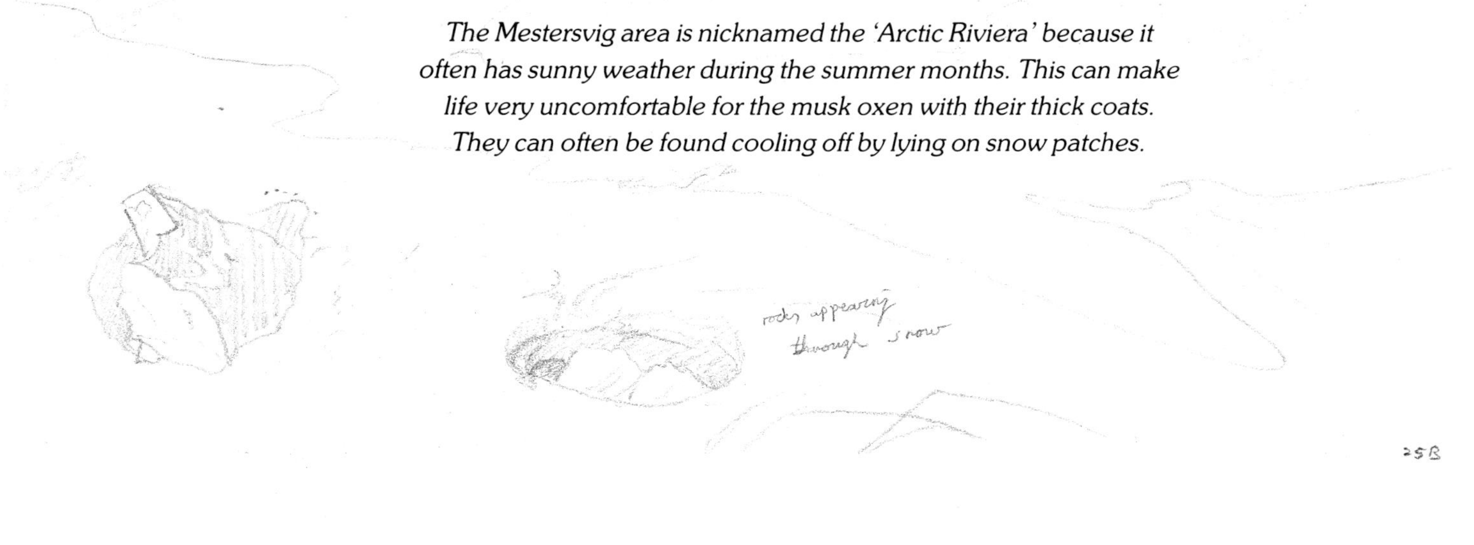

25B

28th July 88

Mestersvig, Greenland 19th August 88

These Arctic foxes are in their summer coat, while in the winter
months they grow a thick white coat. They become increasingly bold
as they forage around the camps for food scraps but their novelty
wears thin at times. In 1988 we had caught a number of Arctic charr
in the Fjord as a treat for expeditioners returning from the mountains
the next day. Overnight all the fish vanished despite being stored
under large blocks of ice floe; no doubt the fox(es) had them cached
somewhere on the nearby hillside.

♂ Snowy Owl
Camperdown Zoo 92

1st winter Gyr Falcon
Nov 92

Cloudberry ½

Heather ½

Crowberry ½

Blaeberry ½

Cowberry ½

Autumn berries found on the hill include the blaeberry, cloudberry, crowberry and cowberry. The blaeberries and crowberries are the most abundant and are favoured by the ptarmigan, as indicated by their purple-black faeces at this time of year. The leaves and shoots of heather, crowberry and blaeberry form the basic diet of the ptarmigan at all seasons, particularly during the winter months.

Philonotis Fontana

20th August 92   1/1

Viola palustris

Sphagnum sp

Frogs are still abundant on the hills. I picked this one up by a wet
mossy spring at 850 metres on the eastern Cairnwell slopes. I have
found their spawn in pools as high as 810 metres on Meall Odhar
just opposite.

Young leverets can be born as late as August but they have much less chance of surviving the winter compared with those maturing from earlier litters. This half-grown leveret was sitting amongst the blaeberry which is already turning red at higher altitude (840 metres in this painting) by late August.

Stag, Harris Bay, Rum 14th Oct 88

Harris Bay, Rum
12th Oct 88

hind basking in sun,
Harris Bay, Rum   14th Oct 88

Red deer sketches from the island of Rum, October 1989.

hind, Harris Bay, Rum   11th Oct 88

Female ptarmigan preening and ruffling their feathers in the November snow. By now they have lost most of their autumn plumage in time for the first real snowfalls of the winter.

Contents

All drawings are reproduced at the same size as the original artwork unless otherwise stated.
The percentages shown indicate the size of the original in relation
to the reproduction.

P   Pencil   WC   Watercolour   CP   Coloured Pencil   A   Acrylic

71	Hare sketches	P	
72	Leveret studies	P, WC	
73	Leveret portraits	P, WC, CP	
74	Peregrine falcon chick	P	
75	Peregrine portraits	P, WC	
76	Wing remains	WC	
77	Eagle chick	P, WC	150%
78	Hare in a form	WC, CP	
79	Hare by a snow fence	WC	
80	Hare sketches	CP	
82	Autumn ptarmigan	WC, CP	150%
84	Northern louded yellow	WC	
85	Merlin chick	WC	150%
86	Harlequin ducks	P, WC	
88	Greenland landscapes	WC	160%
90	Lemmings	P, WC	
92	Snowy owl feathers and pellet	WC	
93	Reindeer antler	WC	
94	Male Greenland ptarmigan	WC	150%
96	Female ptarmigan with chicks	WC	
98	Mountain avens	WC	
99	Arctic poppies	WC	
100	Arctic hare sketches	P	
102	Arctic hare sketches	P, CP	
104	Stretching hares	P, WC	
106	Upright hare	WC	
107	Hare yawning and skull	P, WC	
108	Musk ox sketch	P	
110	Musk oxen in landscape	WC	150%
112	Musk oxen in snow	P	150%
114	Arctic fox details	WC, CP	
116	Snowy Owl	P, WC	
117	Gyr falcon portrait	WC	
118	Autumn berries	WC	
119	Frog	WC	
120	Young hare in autumn	WC	
122	Red deer sketches	P	150%
124	November ptarmigan	WC, CP	150%
128	Mountain hare sketch	P	

Appendix

PLANTS

Alpine Bistor	*Polygonum viviparum*
Alpine Lady's Mantle	*Alchemilla alpina*
Alpine Meadow-rue	*Thalictrum alpinum*
Arctic Poppy	*Papaver radicatum*
Blaeberry	*Vaccinium myrtillus*
Cloudberry	*Rubus chamaemorus*
Cowberry	*Vaccinium vitis-idaea*
Creeping Azalea	*Loiseleuria procumbens*
Crowberry	*Empetrum nigrum agg*
Dwarf Cornel	*Cornus suecica*
Frog Orchid	*Coeloglossum viride*
Heather	*Calluna vulgaris*
Mountain Avens	*Dryas octopetala*
Scottish Aspodel	*Tofieldia pusilla*
Mat Grass	*Nardus stricta*
Sheathed Sedge	*Carex vaginata*
Stiff Sedge	*Carex bigelowii*
Wavy Hair-grass	*Deschampsia flexuosa*
Fir Clubmoss	*Huperzia selago*
Woolly Fringe Moss	*Rhacomitrium lanuginosum*

REPTILES

Common Frog	*Rana temporaria*

MAMMALS

Arctic Fox	*Alopex lagopus*
Arctic Hare	*Lepus arcticus*
Collared (Arctic) Lemming	*Dicrostonyx groenlandicus*
Mountain Hare	*Lepus timidus*
Musk Ox	*Ovibus moschatus*
Norway Lemming	*Lemmus lemmus*
Red Deer	*Cervus elephanus*
Red Fox	*Vulpes vulpes*
Stoat	*Mustela erminea*
Weasel	*Mustela nivalis*

BIRDS

Common Gull	*Larus canus*
Dotterel	*Charadrius morinellus*
Golden Eagle	*Aquila chrysaetos*
Gyr Falcon	*Falco rusticolus candicans*
Harlequin Duck	*Histrionicus histrionicus*
Merlin	*Falco columbaris*
Peregrine Falcon	*Falco peregrinus*
Raven	*Corvus corax*
Red Grouse (Willow Ptarmigan)	*Lagopus lagopus scoticus*
Rock Ptarmigan	*Lagopus mutus*
Snowy Owl	*Nyctea scandiaca*

Meall Odhar, 21st April 90